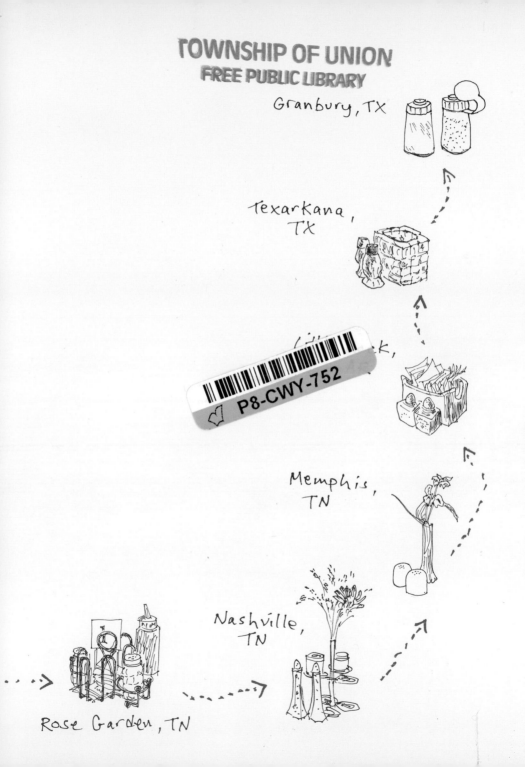

Granbury, TX

Texarkana, TX

Memphis, TN

Nashville, TN

Rose Garden, TN

Cornflakes

Poems by
James Stevenson
with illustrations by the author

Greenwillow Books
An Imprint of HarperCollins*Publishers*

Watercolor paints and a black pen
were used for the full-color art.

Cornflakes: Poems
Copyright © 2000 by James Stevenson
Printed in Hong Kong by South China
Printing Company (1988) Ltd.
http://www.harperchildrens.com

**Library of Congress
Cataloging-in-Publication Data**

Stevenson, James, (date)
Cornflakes : poems /
by James Stevenson.
      p.   cm.
"Greenwillow Books."
Summary: A collection of short
poems with such titles as "I Can't
Move Mountains," "Junkyard,"
and "Greenhouse in March."
ISBN 0-688-16718-7
1. Children's poetry, American.
[1. American poetry.]   I. Title.
PS3569.T4557C67   2000
811'.54—dc21   99-29846   CIP

1 2 3 4 5 6 7 8 9 10
First Edition

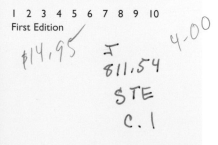

For Jimmy

Contents

Somebody small and brave
Left his Base Camp
At Pink Paper Plate,
Trekked across slippery Green Pickles,
Climbed over the Jagged Chips,
Grabbed an Onion Curl
And swung across to Lower Bun.
He slogged through
Mayo, Mustard, Melted Cheese,

Then crept up Burger Cliff
And on to Upper Bun,
And on the summit proudly stuck
The small blue flag of Cellophane.

In the park
The fathers
Teach the kids
Everything
They'll need to know:

How to catch,

How to throw,

How to hit,

And how to tie their shoes.

Banged-up tables,

Busted sofas,

Chairs with broken arms

 and legs

Wait for Mr. Belfont

(Doctor of furniture)

To make them

Good as new.

TITAN

I'd like to make

One painting

Half as nice

As my paint box

Left alone.

When the wind blows
Through the junkyard
You can hear the hubcaps
Clang.

One day
Our paperwhite narcissus
Declared,
"I am too lovely
And I smell too sweet,"

And swooned.

Packed in ice,

The *Island Queen*

Waits out the winter,

Waiting for July—

For flags,

Warm winds,

And ice cream.

L

oyal and true,
My wastebasket
Says yes to everything.
"NOT BAD! . . . QUITE GOOD! . . .
OH, EXCELLENT! . . .
ARE YOU SURE
YOU DON'T WANT THAT BACK?"

Hard workers,
one and all,
They ratt-
le down
the road together,
Heading for the job.

139   141

"May I borrow

A cup of sugar?"

Calls Number 139.

"Certainly," says 141.

"I'll meet you downstairs."

THERE'S A FACTORY
ON THE POST ROAD.
YOU CAN'T TELL
WHAT IT MAKES.
MAYBE IT
DOESN'T MAKE
ANYTHING.
MAYBE IT JUST
BREATHES IN AND OUT.

Every day
The bent old woman
Shuffles down the sidewalk,
Inch by inch.

From in front,
She has no face.

From behind,
She has no head.

All you see is
Her coat, her cane, her courage.

*O*utside, cold branches
Scrape the glass.
Inside, the jungle
Blooms.

I CAN'T MOVE MOUNTAINS.

I CAN'T STOP THE CLOCK.

I CAN'T CURE THE COMMON COLD.

BUT I CAN MAKE IT SNOW IN CHICAGO.

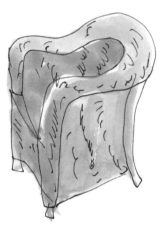

If you go past the

Outdoor furniture shop,

You'll see there is

More than one way

To take a load off.

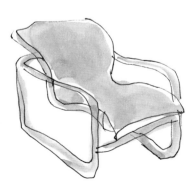

It's Garbage day in the city.

The bags sit on the sidewalk,

Dressed in black,

Wearing bow ties,

READY FOR THE OPERA.

Every day the basket man puts all his baskets out.

Every night the basket man puts all his baskets in.

Along the shore

The perfect shell

Awaits the perfect child.

The Fenders, the Martins,

The Gretsches, the Gibsons

Hang from their hooks

On the music store ceiling,

Waiting for someone

To set their sound free.

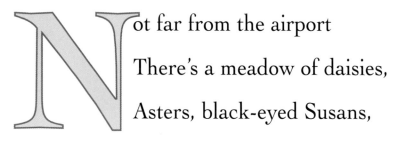

ot far from the airport

There's a meadow of daisies,

Asters, black-eyed Susans,

Buicks, Pontiacs, and Queen Anne's lace.

At the concrete plant
It's feeding time:
The fat white trucks
Crowd in,
Piglets
with
upturned
snouts.

IF YOU ALWAYS WALK
→ STRAIGHT AHEAD
YOU'LL PROBABLY MISS
WHAT'S JUST
AROUND THE
CORNER

All along the island road,

everybody's got a ride,

one way or another.

ffl's TAKE-OUT MENU

APPETIZERS / SIDE DISHES

NEW ENGLAND CLAM CHOWDER

STEAMERS

CHERRY CASINO

MONKFICH MUSSELS

ASSORTED ...

...

LITTLENECKS

...

OYSTERS

...

FRIED CALAMARI

FRIED WHOLE CLAMS

FRIED SCALLOPS

FRIED SHRIMP

FRENCH FRIES

...

SALAD BOWL

SANDWICHES / LIGHT MEALS

FISH ...

SCALLOP ...

LOBSTER ...

TUNA CLUB ...

BLT ...

GRILLED CHICKEN ...

...

...

HAMBURGER

CHEESE ...

OPEN STEAK ...

CHOPPED SIRLOIN

CHEESE ...

LOBSTER ROLL, PLATE

TUNA SALAD ...

...

LINGUINI DISHES

SHRIMP SCAMPI

VEGGIE STIR FRY

SERVED ... / SALADS / ...

WHITE CLAM SAUCE

SUPREME VEGGIE STIR ...

ENTREES W/ ...

FILET MIGNON

ALASKAN CRAB LEGS

BAKED STUFFED ...

BROILED TUNA

COLE SLAW

...

BROILED TWIN LOBSTER

FRIED / SAUTEED SWAI

BROILED ...

SEAFOOD / ... PLATTERS / ...

BROILED ... PLATTER

FRIED FISHERMAN'S PLATTER

WITH ...

FRIED ...

FISH & CHIPS

BROILED LOBSTER

One day last summer
A man stood in front of
The Clam Box
Take-out menu.

"Clam Cakes," he said.
"I'll have Clam Cakes."
Then he said, "No . . .
Fried Shrimp . . . Wait . . .
Lobster Salad . . . No . . .
Filet of Fish . . . Hold it.
Fried Calamari!"

That night, when they closed
The Clam Box windows,
You could still hear his voice
In the dusk:
"Veggie Stir-Fry . . . No . . .
Wait . . .
Salad Bowl . . . !"

It was a foggy day on the island—
Bad luck for visitors who came to see

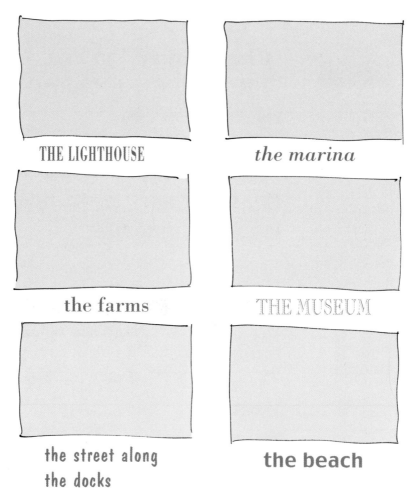

THE LIGHTHOUSE

the marina

the farms

THE MUSEUM

the street along
the docks

the beach

Until . . .
The sun burned through,
And it was a perfect day for visitors.

Salt & Pepper, U.S.A.
A Road Trip Journal

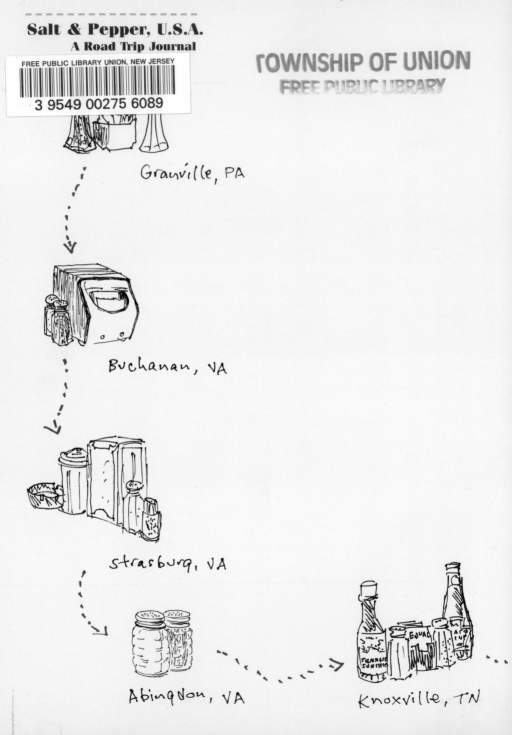

Granville, PA

Buchanan, VA

Strasburg, VA

Abingdon, VA

Knoxville, TN